WINNING THE HEALTH CARE GAME
Save For Your Future!

JONATHAN PIERPONT WARNER, CEBS

**Copyright © 2015 Jonathan Pierpont Warner, CEBS
WINNING THE HEALTH CARE GAME**
ISBN-13: 978-1502485069
ISBN-10: 1502485060
Version: 1.3
All rights reserved. This book has been crafted to be educational with sufficient technical information to act as a reference guide. The characters in the text and their circumstances are fictional. Similarities to actual individuals and families are purely coincidental. The author shall not be liable for any damages or consequences that result from hypothetical projections or effects of using information provided herein and from online references.
No portion may be reproduced or used without written permission of the author, except in a book review of its contents.

"WINNING THE HEALTH CARE GAME" is a condensed version of the original 2013 "HOW TO WIN THE HEALTH CARE GAME."

Jon's BLOG
thehealthcaremind.com

LinkedIn
www.linkedin.com/in/jonathanpwarner

Twitter
www.twitter.com/healthcaremind

Facebook
www.facebook.com/healthcaremind

WHAT PEOPLE ARE SAYING ABOUT
WINNING THE HEALTH CARE GAME

"Educating our employees about changes in healthcare is easier because of this book. It provides a historical background, offers real life examples and clearly explains why it is so important to learn the new definition of great health insurance coverage. This is a must read for all age groups so that unexpected health care costs never become a financial burden. Jon Warner is an expert who cares about the long term financial and medical health of people."
Greg Kelly President Kelly Automotive Group

"I have great respect for Jon Warner resulting from our many years of business collaboration. As a health insurance expert and creative thinker, Jon understands risk and the corresponding cost. In his comprehensive style, Jon details in this book the current state of health care and insurance offering creative insights. I hope you enjoy this book and find it as informative as I have."
Pepper Krach, Communications Practice Leader A. J. Gallagher & Co.

"It took time for our company to embrace the concepts promoted in this book. Once we transitioned, it is the simplicity of the coverage and the opportunity to compare the cost of health care services that has been most eye opening. The answer to high quality, affordable and balanced health insurance is so very well explained in this book, along with ways to build retirement health care savings.

David Weinstein President Sunburst Property Group

"Education about health insurance trends is a daily part of my profession. What Jon Warner offers in his book is refreshing and easy to follow. The concepts he describes are a pathway for excellent protection that help us look at insurance in a new light financially and philosophically. I especially appreciated his people stories as they are realistic and personal."

Vicki L. Doulé Senior Director Capital Blue Cross

"I have successfully introduced the concepts in this book to many employers. They reduce their cost while their employees maintain excellent health insurance coverage and spend less. This book clearly explains how to design quality insurance coverage that is affordable in our changing world."
Matt Hayes Senior Account Executive Sovereign Insurance Group

"**WINNING THE HEALTH CARE GAME** should be mandatory reading for everyone involved in designing health care plan options. Jon Warner describes with great clarity changes occurring with the passage of the Affordable Care Act and includes vivid illustrations of health plan decision making by individuals at different life and economic stages. With the help of Jon's wisdom, an organization I led introduced the ideas presented here and was able to control cost plus adopt wellness standards that accrued to the financial benefit of the corporation and most importantly to the overall well being of our employees and their families."
F. Mark Gumz Retired CEO Olympus of the Americas

WINNING THE HEALTH CARE GAME

JONATHAN PIERPONT WARNER, CEBS

INTRODUCTION

FOREWORD by Kirk A. Putt

Section One – Wisdom for Winning the Health Care Game

I.	Health Insurance Financial Planning	1
II.	Health Insurance History & Inefficient Copays & the Drip vs. Gusher Reality	5
III.	Obamacare Fulfills a Promise, Includes Risk Acceptance & Wellness Standards	13
IV.	Account Based Plans – HSA, FSA, HRA	23
V.	Bargained Plans & Too Much Insurance	39
VI.	Medicare – When I'm 65 or maybe 70	43

Section Two – Winning the Health Care Game
People Stories

VII.	Single Ann's Winning Counselor	51
VIII.	Dave & Doris' Best Choice	57
IX.	Invincible Charlie's Winning Choice	59
X.	Amy & Joe's Mature Analysis	63

Section Three – Efficiently Winning the Health Care Game

XI.	The New Way to Ask Your Doctor	69
XII.	Charge Master Woes & Billing Reform	73
XIII.	The Economics of Health Care & Employment	77
XIV.	Efficiently Winning the Health Care Game	81

Benefits Glossary   89
Blog Link & Online Resources   93
JP Warner Biography   94

Charts & Commentary

1. Annual Frequency of Health Care Services — 1
2. Opportunity for 100% Protection, — 2
3. Milton Friedman on Health Care — 3
4. Health Plan Design Continuum — 8
5. Specialist Office Visit Claim — 9
6. Drip vs. Gusher Linkage — 12
7. Premiums in must be Greater than Payments — 17
8. Hardship Provisions to Avoid Penalties — 18
9. Bio-Metric, Metabolic Standards — 19
10. Affordable Care Act Wealth Redistribution — 22
11. Remember the Acronyms — 23
12. Fourth Leg of the Retirement Stool — 24
13. HSAs Exclusivity Rules — 27
14. HDHP Metallic Plan Comparison — 30

15. Section 125 & Income Taxes	34
16. HRA 1ˢᵗ Dollar Reimbursement	37
17. FSA HRA HSA Maximums	38
18. H. S. A. Growth	41 & 42
19. Medicare Part B, Supp & Rx Premiums	48
20. Qualified High Deductible Plan,	55
21. Ann's Financial Analysis	56
22. Dave & Doris Analysis	58
23. Charlie's Winning Analysis	61
24. Amy & Joe's Analysis	64
25. Sample Health Risk Analysis	66
26. All Truth Goes Through 3 Stages	68
27. Patient Awareness Reduces Spending	71
28. Actual Charges & Discounts	75
29. Best Insurance has Lower Premium	88

INTRODUCTION

Pay attention to the waves when sands shift under foot. The tide is changing for health care insurance coverage standards as the Affordable Care Act (ACA) continues to unfold.

The virtues of the reform law are often offset with stories fanning the flame of it's hoped for demise. Consider though that greater awareness by Americans about the real cost of health insurance is a potential virtue of the law.

Why virtuous? Excessive and wasteful spending slows with this knowledge. And in America, changing historical usage standards is critical to saving our high quality health care system.

This book offers perspectives on the ACA law while avoiding the hills and valleys of opinion to explain:

1. How we got to this crossroad.
2. Opportunities to come out ahead.
3. Why there is time to prepare for our future.

Building a health care reserve is a new reality and a recent concept, likely to take over as the standard for comprehensive protection. It is not perfect, as concern will always be present about lack of affordability for out of pocket risk exposure, and unwillingness to part with savings as an excuse for avoidung timely and important medical help.

 And yet it makes sense to plan for future health care needs while younger, when considering life span expectations for the many of us. Studies confirm that if you make it to age 65, on average you will live until age 86 if male and 89 if female.

If you've studied Medicare Parts A&B, then you are surprised by its limitations. It's not generous. Current retirees spend between $2,500 & $8,000 per person per year in premiums, plus pay money out of pocket when receiving care. And, higher income plus living longer adds to retiree health insurance costs.

Too many of us consider only the cost of health care expenses that may happen today, tomorrow, or over the course of the next 12 months.

Why this short term thinking?

Just like with cars and homes, more expensive means better, right? Wrong. Because of the Affordable Care Act, also known as Obamacare, lower premium plans now offer the same level of unlimited catastrophic health care protection as more costly coverage. Your annual out of pocket risk is limited by law.

It's better to pay higher premiums so I have minimal copay cost when I visit my physician, pick up a prescription or have a test performed, right? Not anymore. Insurance companies can tack on 15% to 20% on top of every premium dollar and the government adds another 4.5%

to 5% in taxes. For the convenience of having the insurance company pay $100, expect a $25 surcharge in your premiums. The smaller the convenient copay, the more it costs overall.

With the introduction of Healthcare Marketplace Exchanges for individuals, selecting a plan now starts with understanding the full premium cost and then subtracting, if your income is low enough, available monetary subsidies provided by the government.

The new world of health insurance selection includes consideration of:

1. Total premium expense
2. Net personal premium cost
3. Out of pocket risk exposure

Fortunately most of us have an inconsistent need for costly health care services each year. What follows is a roadmap for maintaining quality and affordable insurance protection that allows tax efficient savings to be used for normal care needs.

All of us are likely to take advantage of health care services during our lifetime and most have already benefitted from the system if born in a hospital. The list of curative services available today is awe inspiring compared with one generation ago, and we should anticipate more amazing advancements in the years to come. This may be the most important reason for you to build a reserve while healthy.

Jon Warner *January 2015*

FOREWORD

As president of a company employing 300 and insuring almost 600 individuals, I know the power of health care. Finding the right balance between this multi-million dollar expense and the best care options for employees and their families is a major challenge – one that requires expertise to navigate.

Jon Warner has provided that guidance to countless companies and their employees for over 30 years. Following 14 years in the insurance industry, Jon started his business, JP Warner Associates, Inc. in 1997 to service companies' employee benefit needs. He has been a leader and champion of Consumer Driven Health Plans and creative plan designs.

Jon has a unique ability to sift through the deluge of ever-changing health care legislation and trendy acronyms to provide real world meaning in layman's terms. He does so with the perspective of someone deeply rooted in faith who always remembers behind every medical expense there is a life being impacted.

Jon and I share a very personal connection to this topic. Both Jon and my mother had successful life-saving surgery performed by the same surgeon at Jefferson University Hospital in Philadelphia. They were both blessed to have access and financial means to get the best care available in the world.

Whether you are a business owner, manager, hourly worker, or unemployed, you can benefit from the guidance provided in this book. Serious health conditions do not discriminate and when they occur, we all want to be in a position to get the best care.

We face significant changes in our health care system due to the PPACA legislation, also known as the Affordable Care Act and Obamacare. I tell our employees openly that I do not have a perfect solution to eliminate rising medical expenses, nor does the government; however, I strongly believe in Jon Warner's premise that an educated medical consumer with financial ownership will make better decisions for themselves and their family than executives and politicians.

Kirk A. Putt
President & CEO R-V Industries, Inc.

Dedicated to the memory of **Edwin T. Johnson** (1930 – 2012), the Founder and CEO of The Johnson Companies, Newtown, PA. Ed's intellect, communication skills and confidence has inspired many of his fellow Americans to plan for their future.

Background for Winning the Health Care Game

I. Health Insurance Financial Planning

A winning strategy is catching on to best afford highly desirable, yet expensive American health care. The change that is taking hold across America includes accepting short term risk to free up dollars that allow for longer term savings.

The truth is that most people have an inconsistent need for high cost health care, and yet we define excellent health insurance as coverage that minimizes how much we must spend out of our pockets when we need care.

We are too easily swayed to justify spending more on health insurance because it is complicated when sorting out value. And yet, no risk, peace of mind unfortunately has become less and less affordable.

ANNUAL FREQUENCY OF HEALTH CARE SERVICES

- 15% of us incur no health care costs
- 60% of us use normal health care services such as Office visits & Rx
- 25% of us require high cost health care such as Hospitalization, Surgery, X-ray & Laboratory services

Even though our inconsistent need for high cost care seems like it cannot be well quantified or communicated due to life's risks, winners are looking long term, embracing health insurance that covers all high cost needs and paying out of pocket for normal care needs with premium savings.

Fortunately there is a tax favored way to build a health care savings reserve with investment options similar to a 401k or 403b savings plan used for retirement. Even better, funds spent from the account are never taxed if used for qualified health care services. Yes, never taxed!

It was only 100 years ago that most people passed away before they reached age 60. Today, 60 is the new age 40 with many of us anticipating living into our 90's or even to 100!

The opportunity continues for most of us to have 100% of our future health care needs paid in full in order to win the health care game. It comes down to building equity while accepting reasonable risk.

Many societal advances catch on because they reduce risk, although it is never completely eliminated. Bringing along an umbrella, raincoat and boots on a day when heavy downpours are expected is prudent. When the forecast calls for occasional showers and may mean getting wet, lugging along extra gear to avoid the risk is usually not worth it. This context merits consideration regarding many of life's opportunities and trade-offs, including health insurance coverage selection.

Adding to the efficiency rationale is a truism about how having some skin in the game impacts decision making. **Milton Friedman** is remembered as a brilliant economist. He summarized well why health insurance should include personal out of pocket risk:

> # "No one spends someone else's money as carefully as their own."

II. Health Insurance History, Inefficient Copays & the Drip vs. Gusher Reality

The history of America's private and public health insurance system is less than 100 years old, dating back to the 1930's. To stabilize revenue and to grow, hospitals banded together to form <u>Hospital Service Plans</u>. Using the concept of insurance, a nominal premium was charged to many, guaranteeing 100% payment for limited number of hospital care days.

By spreading the cost to a large group, individual citizens paid a small premium, which covered the expense of the ever-changing 11 percent of the population whose health care needs require treatment in a hospital setting. Hospital Service Plans, which were rebranded as Blue Cross Plans, took time to catch on.

Extensive growth occurred in the 1940's as employers agreed to pay premiums for their workers to enhance compensation during the wage and price control period necessitated by World War II. Tax deductible employer paid insurance soon became an accepted cost of doing business and a valued benefit to workers.

In 1946 the Hill- Burton Act became law offering funding, including grants and loans to expand and build new hospitals across the United States. Care provided free to low income, uninsured Americans was required.

By the 1950's more sophisticated and specialized physician care became available, with Blue Shield plans spreading the risk of in-patient physician services.

With the addition of Major Medical coverage in the 1960's, comprehensive insurance coverage including office visits and prescription costs became available.

The HMO Act of 1973 promulgated a pre-payment system to providers of care so they accepted liability for managing reoccurring health care needs. HMOs originally eliminated deductibles and coinsurance in favor of nominal, flat copays per visit. HMOs established contractual relationships with hospitals and doctors to share risk in the treatment of patients.

HMO plans also included preventive care services to promote good health. They contrasted with traditional insurance plans that were truly "sick insurance" plans that paid only if a diagnosis confirmed an illness or accident.

Copays formed the basis of the late 20th century "Managed Care" era including HMOs (Health Maintenance Organizations), PPOs (Preferred Provider Organizations) and POS (Point of Service) plans.

Reductions in personal, out of pocket responsibility for health care became the new standard. A generation of Americans grew up used to paying very little out of pocket when accessing health care services.

America's aging population and the ever increasing number of available and government mandated health care services then led to year upon year of increasing premium costs. This prompted employers to charge employees increasingly higher amounts from paychecks in order to maintain pre-paid, low out of pocket health insurance coverage.

In time deductibles and out of pocket responsibility also increased. By 2002 rules were released allowing Health Reimbursement Arrangements (HRA) to limit personal cost exposure from high deductibles and coinsurance.

Legislation signed in 2003 introduced Health Savings Accounts (HSA). These are pre-tax savings plans like IRAs were restricted to individuals enrolled in a Qualified High Deductible Health Plan (HDHP).

Flexible Spending Accounts (FSA), first enacted in 1978 allow participants to pay personal health care costs on a pre-tax basis, grew in favor thanks to access to the entire annual deferral at time of need. Rolling over unspent amounts up to $500 was added in 2013.

Since premium costs are tax deductible to employers, historical tendencies have been toward pre-paid coverage plans that pay for normal care needs, maximizing peace of mind and perceived "best coverage," This was health coverage Nirvana until premiums became unaffordable for more and more of Americans.

Health Plan Design Continuum

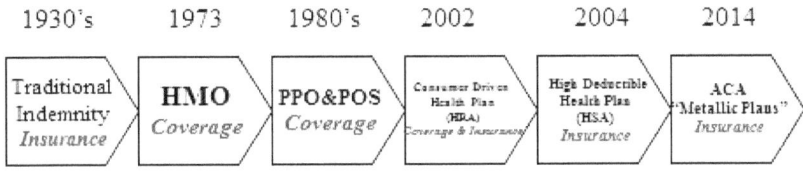

Ever higher premium costs have emerged to pay for:

1. Excess Utilization - Minimal personal cost responsibility that too often translates to redundant and ever increasing health care service usage.

2. Administrative Overhead - Think about it in terms of percentages. The insurance company adds 15% - 20% to rates for overhead and profit, plus state and federal taxes can add another 4.5% - 5%.

3. Hyper inflated Charges - Confusion caused by the difference between charges and discounted covered amounts.

Although it is unusual in our free market economy to make a purchase without regard to its cost, this occurs when patient responsibility is limited to copays, as they mask the real cost of health care services. And yet copays are convenient. Paying flat copays ($20, $40, $100) per health care service event and remain the standard in today's Platinum level health plans.

Specialist Office Visit Example
$150 Specialist Visit
$50 Copay & $100 Insurance Payment
$25 Administration & Taxes added to premium
$175 Total Cost
Or, Upfront Deductible Plan
$150 Payment with HRA or HSA
$0 Insurance Payment
$0 Administrative fee in premium
$150 Total Cost

As health premium increases outpace inflation year after year, advocates of cost efficiency have considered whether copays are the appropriate mechanism for cost sharing. Before HMOs, PPOs, & POS plans, health insurance included deductibles, coinsurance and daily coverage limits.

Lower premiums are charged for plans that include deductibles and coinsurance versus copay plans, as risk is transferred to the patient. Cost awareness increases the patient's sense of value and selection.

Since just 11% of our population is hospitalized each year, coverage for this type of protection merits including risk acceptance. And yet, since a hospital experience can result in many thousands of dollars in cost it may seem counter intuitive to accept financial risk for such an expensive circumstance.

Think about how many days you have been a hospital inpatient as compared to the days you have been alive. How often do you carry an umbrella when the chance of rain is less than 20%?

A traditional way to temper premium increases while keeping patients in touch with the cost of health care is the acceptance of coinsurance. After a deductible is satisfied, insurance pays 50% to 90% of costs to an "out of pocket" maximum. It's important to grasp the out-of-pocket cap, where 90% or 70% or 50% in coverage transitions to 100% coverage. With 10% coinsurance of a $50,000 bill, one accepts $5,000 in out of pocket risk.

The Affordable Care Act allows risk exposure up to $6,450 in 2015 for a single HDHP. Remembering that all health insurance plans eventually pay 100% of costs prompts efficiency options to take risk, lower premiums and use pre-tax FSAs & HSAs to pay for risk exposure.

"DRIP" VERSUS "GUSHER" MENTALITY

Protection from an unaffordable financial health care cost "Gusher" is the most important reason to be insured. Minimizing personal cost responsibility with plans that have low copays is based on a premise that too few Americans have emergency resources.

Let's presume you are responsible for the first $2,000 of cost if admitted to the hospital. While this is a lot of money if living from paycheck to paycheck, consider how it compares financially to the cost of smoking a pack of cigarettes per day. Pack a day smokers spend more than $2,000 per year.

It is intriguing how we place a different financial value on "Gusher" risk versus the daily purchase of "death sticks", which include cigarettes and salty high fat foods like greasy French fries. To reinforce the point, the cost to buy lunch at fast food restaurants now averages around $9 per meal. If purchased every work day over 50 weeks, that annual outlay is $2,250.

In America we culturally support a "Drip Mentality" approach to cash flow. Our drip deductions from gross earnings can be so significant that we learn to live on a net amount that is up to 50% less than full pay when taxes, insurance and retirement savings payroll deductions are added together.

DRIP VS GUSHER LINKAGE

Why not Drip your own money into a Flexible Spending Account or Health Savings Account so you have emergency funds when Gusher health care costs occur?

III. <u>Obamacare Fulfills a Promise, Includes Risk Acceptance & Wellness Standards</u>

Healthy citizens add to our country's competitive edge in the global market place. Workers are most productive when they feel well. This is not discussed often enough by business leaders as a reason why health insurance is offered as a benefit to employees. Park your pre-conceived notions about Obamacare and think objectively about these questions:

1. Should employers who do not invest in the health care needs of their workers be required to pay into a fund to assist their employees to purchase their own health insurance protection?

2. Should part time workers, the disabled and retirees have access to the same level of insurance protection as fulltime workers?

3. Since many purchases occur today utilizing the power of the Internet, why not health insurance?

Long term planners foresee a time when all Americans will go online to select a health insurance plan of their choice. Prices will be based upon age, income and the amount of pre-paid services built into the coverage. Private insurance companies will accept all applicants regardless of their health history.

Business owners, union leaders, financial and human resource executives will no longer decide on plan choices. Employers and employees will no longer look at health insurance as an unpredictable budget item.

This may come true as the foundation for such a development has been rolling out since President Barack Obama signed legislation that was voted for along Democratic Party lines to massively change the American health care system. The well-intentioned goal of uniform health insurance coverage for all Americans finally, after many attempts spanning decades, culminated in 2010 when the Patient Protection & Affordable Care Act (PPACA) became law.

The framework for personalized health insurance purchase along with tighter quality of care by hospitals and doctors will hopefully serve future generations of Americans well. Long overdue insurance rules in the law require acceptance by an insurer if pre-existing medical conditions exist, plus offer parents' the ability to insure children until age 26.

Unlimited payments to allow the chronically ill to never exhaust their overall financial resources plus 100% preventive care coverage add to this comprehensive law.

Since the uninsured cost of spending more than a day in the hospital can equal the price of a new automobile and result in personal bankruptcy, these are welcome protections. It is all great if affordable and not overly bureaucratic.

A GARGANTUAN CHALLENGE
Obamacare includes new taxes, reduces Medicare spending and expands government oversight, plus introduces penalties for those not insured. Employers with 50+ workers not offering insurance must pay into a fund to help subsidize the individual purchase of insurance. These are well publicized, gargantuan challenges to the success of the legislation, so significant to merit a Supreme Court ruling.

The law addresses health care delivery standardization, for better or the opposite. New plan design standards and premium rates are revolutionary. Optimistic proponents argue the incentives and disincentives in The Affordable Care Act increase efficiency while maintaining quality standards and reducing costs. Time will tell if this new thinking is accepted as in everyone's best interests.

Health care consumption begins when patients seek care and treatment for accidents, illnesses and diseases. Physicians sign orders for every diagnostic health care dollar that is spent. Changing payment standards and incentives is a part of The Affordable Care Act, transitioning from fee for service to bundled payments to providers of care for restoring patient health. The hospitals and doctors have no choice but to bear increased financial and quality risk.

HEALTH INSURANCE FOR ALL
A primary goal of The Affordable Care Act is to add 30 million more Americans to health insurance rolls as a

form of social justice. Questions include whether all Americans benefit from this expansion as it will challenge physician and hospital resources. One concern is that the newly insured may strain the system because of a spike in demand for medical services. The maturation of PPACA raises many questions:

- Have increased utilization projections for the newly insured been properly accounted for?
- Will there be enough physicians and support personnel to provide quality services?
- Will new regulatory restrictions on health insurance companies allow proper rate setting to cover costs?
- Are additional tax increases inevitable to subsidize the true cost of expanded coverage?

Under The Affordable Care Act the maximum payroll deduction allowed for workers is 9.5% of pay. If you earn $40,000 per year, the cap is $3,800 or $146 per bi-weekly pay, a significant rise above national norms.

The high cost of health insurance is becoming better known due to the law, shocking many at just how expensive it is to be well insured. As full premiums become known, an increased acceptance of risk before insurance kicks in is inevitable to maintain affordability.

Subsidies, which are type of tax credit for individuals are significant if annual income falls at or below 200% of the poverty line. Review the following chart to gain a clear sense of premium costs based upon age and the net cost per month based upon one's income.

PENALTY TAX TOO LOW

It may surprise you that 75% of us do not incur substantial health care costs each year. This truth challenges compliance with The Affordable Care Act for Americans voluntarily purchasing coverage. It is more expensive to purchase subsidized health coverage than to accept the Penalty Tax for not buying insurance.

In 2016, a couple earning $40,000 will likely be able to purchase a mid-level Silver plan for about $200 per month, or $2,400 annually once the government subsidy is subtracted from the true premium cost. Their Penalty Tax is $500 in 2014, $1,000 in 2015 and caps out at $1,390, or 58% of subsidized premiums in 2016. Since the plan available at this premium will include significant deductibles and copays, remaining uninsured may still seem the better financial choice.

Insurance only works if premiums paid in are greater than claims costs going out. As premiums rise for the sick people who buy insurance, even the marginally ill may opt out, pressuring the government to legislate more taxes to cover the shortfall.

The PPACA law does not allow wage garnishment or the ability to place a lien on personal property. The Penalty Tax for being uninsured is collected annually at tax time by reducing expected refunds, versus health insurance premiums that must be paid each month.

Hardship exceptions allowing the Penalty Tax to be waived include:

Hardship Provisions to Avoid Penalties

1. Unexpected costs due to caring for an ill family member
2. Substantial debt from medical expenses in last 24 months
3. Financial hardship due to a significant rise in premiums
4. Filed for bankruptcy in last six months
5. Substantial damages to personal property
6. Shut off notice from utility company
7. Eviction, home foreclosure or homeless
8. Victim of domestic violence
9. Recent death of a family member
10. Child who should be covered by a parent
11. During an eligibility appeal period applying for coverage
12. Too challenged by technology details to properly enroll

The ACA premium rating system automatically increases rates each year simply due to growing older. It will challenge coverage affordability, getting ahead and maintaining other than catastrophic insurance protection as we age. Did the planners who designed the system consider these consequences?

It is a wonder why the Penalty Tax became such a lightning bolt issue, rising to the U.S. Supreme Court to affirm its validity. Medicare uses a proven approach to maximize voluntarily participation. The Medicare penalty is effective because if you do not sign up for insurance when first eligible your premiums include a surcharge when enrolled later.

It costs more to delay. A future penalty approach including late enrollment surcharges similar to

Medicare, with caps on premium increases is a worthy alternative to the Obamacare Penalty Tax.

WELLNESS STANDARDS
Exercise and moderate consumption enhances quality of life and saves money on health care. A few French fries, candy and cookies keep life from being bland, and totally eliminating cake and ice cream is not required. And the numbers to beat are not unreasonable for most of us.

Bio-Metric, Metabolic Standards

1. **Cholesterol <200 mg/dl; LDL <130; HDL >40**
2. **Glucose <100 mg/dl**
3. **Blood Pressure <140 systolic <90 diastolic**
4. **Body Mass Index <30 kg./m2**
5. **Carbon Monoxide <5 parts per million**

After a four hour fast, a small amount of blood is drawn by a technician who is able in 20 minutes to report cholesterol and glucose levels. While the analysis is in progress, other tests are administered along with a confidential discussion about health history and lifestyle habits. If any of the numbers are beyond an acceptable range, counseling is provided with the goal of promoting change.

Another test opportunity may occur six to twelve months in the future to gauge progress. The incentive may be rewarded for maintaining three or more of these standards. Or, an incentive is awarded per standard maintained. The point is that all of these levels are controllable through diet, avoidance, exercise and at times diligently taking one's prescribed medicines.

Obamacare allows up to a 30% of single premium incentive for programs designed to reduce and prevent undesirable effects from unhealthy lifestyle standards. It also allows up to a 50% premium surcharge for smoking!

When employers invest in health & wellness programs it positively impacts the bottom line by increasing work attendance and quality of output. The bottom line goal is to reduce health care costs.

To keep cars and trucks running, periodic maintenance is a necessity. The same concept applies to personal health. Try visiting the onsite clinic at work and take advantage of preventive exams covered by your health plan. Or schedule a preventive physical exam with your doctor, paid at 100%. Mammograms at age 40 and colonoscopies at age 50 are proven lifesavers, and are 100% covered in ACA non grandfathered health insurance plans.

Re-occurring telephonic and email outreach by nurses plus face to face wellness coaching at the worksite yields a worthy return on investment. This system of POPULATION HEALTH MANAGEMENT becomes personal, assisting "at risk" employees. It also often spills over to the home, positively affecting spouse and children health habits.

Promoting a combination of daily physical activity, moderation in food and alcohol consumption, the elimination of tobacco consumption and periodic health checkups reduces "risk factors" and their expense. Good habits can be even further supported with stress reduction through Spirituality with a sense of faith and hope. Peace of mind is good for productivity and our sense of purpose.

Incentives by some are considered disincentives to others. If an employer increases payroll contributions for health insurance and then waives the increase for the healthier participants, or offers extra deposits to Health Savings Accounts, Flexible Spending Accounts or a Health Reimbursement Arrangement for those with successful test results, this may be perceived as a stick and not a carrot.

With all of these observations, both positive and critical, applaud that for the first time in America a worker who gets sick or hurt and loses their job can continue to be insured for health care needs at a reasonable cost. This is a wonderful expression of our compassionate society, and if establishing a health care savings fund while healthy emerges as an expected personal responsibility of American citizens, this type of reserve will enhance long term health insurance affordability for all.

> ## "THE AFFORDABLE CARE ACT"
> **Obamacare is a wealth redistribution law. It makes expensive health care affordable for Americans not fortunate enough to have subsidized health insurance coverage through employment. All Americans with employer provided insurance share in the wealth redistribution cost by paying fees & taxes built into premiums. In addition, higher income earners pay more in personal income taxes allowing lower income individuals to purchase financially subsidized insurance from health care marketplace exchanges.**

IV. Account Based Plans – HSA, FSA & HRA

Americans with an inconsistent need for health care services are taught to purchase insurance anticipating near term catastrophe. The Affordable Care Act is unfortunately silent on personal savings for future health care needs. At least though, it did little to change Health Savings Accounts, plus clarified rules for Health Reimbursement Arrangements, and ultimately helped with allowing up to $500 in Flexible Spending Accounts deferrals to roll over to the next plan year.

Remember the Acronyms by Dropping the First & Last Words:

1. **SAVINGS for HSA** (long term build up)
2. **SPENDING for FSA** (must be spent with max $500 rollover)
3. **REIMBURSEMENT for HRA** (from the employer)

HEALTH SAVINGS ACCOUNTS (HSA)

Every year since their availability in 2004, the number of Americans with HSAs has increased. Appreciation and acceptance of HSAs requires a paradigm shift from "renting" insurance protection versus coverage protection that builds "equity and ownership." Building a Health Savings Account balance is a winning strategy.

You have likely heard about HSAs but maybe never dug into why people set them up. Once it is clarified that Health Savings Accounts (HSA) may only be funded if enrolled in a federally qualified High Deductible Health Plan (HDHP), there is lost interest. Another challenge is that since they are "savings" accounts, the build-up of funds occurs over time. HSAs protect cash flow only after there are adequate funds saved in the account. Pre-tax deposit amounts to HSAs are also capped annually. Still, HSAs are becoming the next facet of sound retirement planning.

FOURTH LEG OF THE RETIREMENT STOOL

1. Social Security
2. Retirement Plan Savings
3. Personal Savings including equity in a home
4. *Health Savings Account*

High Deductible Health Plan (HDHP) enrollment is required to fund an HSA. HDHPs on first impression are not considered "good coverage" because of their low premium cost and all diagnostic services subject to satisfaction of an upfront deductible. Nothing is paid by the insurance company for diagnostic care needs.

And yet, coupled with premium savings deposited into an HSA to pay for normal care expenses, the combination offers better long term protection. Since most of us have an inconsistent need for expensive health care services, combining low cost premiums with pre-tax savings for future health care needs allows for building an account to eliminate cash flow risk.

The deductible and coinsurance layer of patient financial responsibility also prompts scrutinization of the cost and value of health care purchases. While maximizing awareness of the real cost of health care services, it is most appreciated by accounting oriented consumers, yet confusing and frustrating to others.

The entire discounted cost of sickness related office visits and prescriptions are subject to the HDHP deductible. Services are "covered", but the insurance does not "pay" until the deductible has been met.

The family deductible is "aggregate", which means that one or multiple family members may accumulate expenses to satisfy the entire deductible. All but preventive care services accumulate towards satisfying the deductible.

Once deductible amounts are paid out, plans cover 100%, 90%, 70% or 50% of additional medical expenses until the participant reaches a final threshold, or "annual out of pocket" maximum. At that time the HDHP insurance plan pays 100% of covered health care costs for the balance of the plan year. HDHPs include 100% coverage for expensive, catastrophic health care costs, as do all Obamacare approved plans.

HDHP participants have the option of opening a personally owned Health Savings Account (HSA). Deposits to the account are not taxed as income. HSA funds may be invested to earn interest that is not taxed, and unused balances roll over to future years. HSA account owners have the opportunity to build savings to offset future health care out-of-pocket costs. While there are limits to the amount of money that may be deposited annually into an HSA, there is no cap on lifetime HSA savings.

Employers may deposit funds into employee HSAs to reduce deductible and out-of-pocket risk. For money to be deposited into an HSA, an individual must be insured <u>only</u> by an HDHP. It is important to maintain the context that rules and restrictions regarding tax savings in this arrangement focus on pre-tax Health Savings Accounts (HSAs).

Legally it is possible for an individual to be covered under an HDHP and a traditional health plan at the same time. If this is the case though, they may not deposit pre-tax funds into an HSA.

HRAs and FSAs, reviewed in detail in the next section may be used instead of HSAs to limit out of pocket exposure, but may not be used in tandem with funding HSAs to pay for medical and prescription expenses until a minimum deductible has been paid in full.

Think about HSAs as having exclusivity rules. They must stand on their own. The positives are striking:
1. Deposits are not taxed as income.
2. HSA money is the property of the account owner.
3. HSA accounts are portable if changing jobs or retiring.
4. Upon death funds pass to a beneficiary.

Rules enhancing the flexibility and value of Health Savings Accounts were released in 2007. These clarifications advanced opportunities for HSA account owners to save more money on a pre-tax basis for post-retirement health care expenses. Adjustments included:

A. Allowing annual deposits up to $1,000 per year as a catch up provision for participants at least age 55 until enrolled in Medicare.

B. The "Last Month" rule allowing a full year tax deduction for HSA money deposited at any time during the calendar year until April 15 of the following year, assuming the participant maintains HDHP coverage.

C. Account holders may add funds up to the legal annual maximum to reimburse themselves for care incurred if an existing HSA balance is less than the amount of health care expenses incurred the date care was received. HDHP coverage must continue for 12 months following such deposits to avoid penalties.

D. Employers have the option to deposit more money into an HSA for lower paid personnel than highly compensated employees.

E. Individual IRA transfers are allowed once per lifetime into an HSA. This opportunity negates having to pay taxes in the future on IRA savings used for qualified health care expenses.

Regardless of one's age, payments from an HSA avoid taxation and penalties if used for federally qualified health expenses under Section 213d, plus for Medicare Advantage Plan premiums and for Long Term Care insurance. HSA money is never taxed if used to pay for qualified health care expenses. What is not spent in a year earns tax-free interest and rolls over to the next year. Income, interest, and usage taxation are avoided.

Prior to age 65, if HSA deposits are used to pay for purchases other than qualified health expenses, the account owner is responsible to pay a 20% penalty along with income taxes. Post age 65 there is no longer a penalty spending savings on non-health care purchases. If used for normal retirement needs then income taxes apply. Upon death, unused HSA money is passed to a spouse as beneficiary who is afforded the same tax treatment as the original account holder.

HSAs are offered with a Debit Card to pay for health care services. Personally maintaining receipts for six years is required by law if ever audited. Third party substantiation of expenditures is not required. Self-management adds to the value of HSAs.

COMMITMENT CONTRACT
There is a way to design an HDHP and HSA by increasing payroll deductions. Presenting two or three payroll deduction options that include additional Health Savings Account funding engages people to consider HSAs. "Commitment Contracts" are forced savings plans and allow price point comparison with higher premium plans.

Proper disclosure is paramount to the Commitment Contract strategy. Questions and comments may arise that an employer is not "giving up anything" by offering higher payroll deductions to fund an HSA at an increased level.

Value enhancement will definitely occur if an employer pre-funds 50% or more of the annual HSA amount at the beginning of the plan year. The point is that HDHP and HSA plans may be offered with multiple contribution levels.

Since additional payroll deduction amounts are voluntary they may be adjusted up or down during the year. This approach maximizes flexibility as deferrals may be stopped if other financial responsibilities arise.

> **HDHP METALLIC PLAN COMPARISON**
> **Platinum – HSA Funded to IRS max**
> **Gold – HSA Fund to 80%**
> **Silver – HSA Fund to 70%**
> **Bronze – HSA Fund to 60%**
> HSA deposits will grow and roll over after a year or two of forced savings for infrequent users of high cost health care services. Future deductible and out of pocket risk is then eliminated. Accepting risk has a limited time horizon.

FLEXIBLE SPENDING ACCOUNTS (FSA)
Flexible Spending Accounts (FSA), a Section 125 benefit, allows the pre-tax payment of qualified health expenses as outlined in Section 213d of the Internal Revenue Code. For many years FSAs enjoyed limited interest because of the "use it or lose it rule", included by lawmakers so that participants accepted risk to pay for health care costs pre-tax.

In October 2013, rules released allowing up to $500 in unused FSA deferrals to roll over to the next plan year. Employers must amend their plans to take advantage, necessitating elimination of the 2.5 month extension to spend unused FSA deferrals.

Significant growth in FSA participation has occurred since 2005 due to the two and a half month reimbursement extension. The ability to pay pre-tax for many "Over the Counter" products and therapies also increased FSA awareness and participation. Unfortunately the Affordable Care Act stripped FSAs of this feature unless physicians write a prescription for Over the Counter products.

Debit card technology that allows ease of payment for FSA purchases, and the "<u>uniform coverage</u>" rule requiring employers to fund annual deferral amounts "at time of need" prior to full collection of FSA funds, adds to the appeal of these accounts. A tax-free, interest-free "loan" is afforded participants that spend their annual FSA deferral early in the year.

FSAs also allow for the upfront payment of scheduled services such as orthodontia treatment. In addition, Debit cards may be loaded with after tax funds for employees desiring forced savings to pay for additional out of pocket health care costs.

The IRS requires substantiation documentation that FSA funds have been used only for qualified Section 213d expenses. Follow up substantiation paperwork must be sent to the FSA administrator, generally within 30 days of a debit card purchase. If not provided, the debit card will stop working unless the participant agrees to reimburse unauthorized usage or have an after tax payroll deduction to reimburse their employer.

Auto-Substantiation can fortunately occur at times thanks to electronic approval standards. The Inventory Information Approval System (IIAS) allows for electronic approvals including flat copayments and reoccurring qualified expenses at the same cost.

DRIP IN WITH GUSHER OUT PROTECTION

Income "drips" from every paycheck to fund an FSA, while 100% of the annual amount promised is available at time of need. A leap of faith is necessary to appreciate FSA Section 125 plan tax savings. The tax benefit shows up in one's paycheck, because the Section 125 deduction is "above the line." So a $100 per pay deferral reduces one's paycheck by $70 on average.

Repeat FSA users are drawn to participate again and again once "gusher" payments are received for the annual amount set aside. When $1,500 or more is needed to satisfy a health insurance deductible, and all of the funds are "on the card", cash flow is protected. Having one's paycheck reduced $30 every week, with net take home pay adjusted down $20, resulting in access to $1,500 when needed, exemplifies how the FSA acts as a wonderful cash flow tool.

At plan year-end, unused FSA amounts are considered "experience gains" for the employer and may be used to offset administrative expenses, or returned to employees in a reasonable and uniform basis. Unsubstantiated FSA expenses may generate a future year W-2 taxable responsibility. The Affordable Care Act limits FSA deferrals to a maximum of $2,550 per worker in 2015.

Unfortunately for some FSAs do not "sizzle." Paychecks include so many deductions today that voluntarily adding another reduction to take home pay is not attractive, even if pre-tax.

Sub Chapter S Corporation owners, directors and partners are not allowed to participate in FSAs. Discrimination rules requiring annual tests to confirm that highly compensated employees do not defer more than lower paid employees is a responsibility in managing FSAs.

Pre-tax deferrals for parking or transit costs and dependent care may be offered as part of an FSA. These deferral options are often included alongside medical care FSA plans. Maximum annual pre-tax deferrals for parking and transit approach changes over time.

Dependent care deferrals up to $5,000 are allowed for joint tax return filers. Access to these funds is limited to deposits made, or "money in, money out." Vendors must provide their Tax ID number in order for parents to take advantage of these non-health care FSAs.

Limited and post-deductible FSAs may be offered in tandem with Health Savings Accounts (HSAs) and allow pre-tax payment of qualified medical services once the HSA minimum legal qualified high deductible has been satisfied, equal to $1,300 single and $2,600 with dependents.

First dollar dental and vision payments can be made from limited FSAs. This is of special value to parents of children with orthodontia expenses. HSA owners who don't want non-medical costs to deplete their HSA balance are attracted to limited FSAs.

HSAs & FSAs Tax Savings Example

- **FIT (Federal)** 18%
- **FICA** 7.65%
- **State** 3.35%
- **Local** 1%
- **Total** 30%

$30 saved in taxes for every $100 spent pre-tax

HEALTH REIMBURSEMENT ARRANGEMENTS

A proven cost efficiency opportunity is available with Health Reimbursement Arrangements (HRA). These are employer offered plans that reimburse participants for a portion of out of pocket costs. HRAs have been available since 2002 and are often referred to as Health Reimbursement Accounts.

Employers who introduce upfront deductible plans often implement HRAs to reimburse a portion of insurance plan deductibles.

One must think retrospectively to embrace the rationale for HRAs. A $100 deductible 30 years ago has about the same value as a $1,000 deductible today. Employers that implement higher deductible plans use an HRA to "back-fill" a portion of employee out-of-pocket exposure.

HRAs help reduce health care expenses in that:

1. Lower claims costs result from plans with upfront deductibles. This translates to reduced premiums.
2. Awareness of the value and cost of health care products and services increases for participants with HRAs.
3. Because 30% to 60% of the promised HRA benefit is used, employers offer a more generous first dollar benefit to employees than with HMO,

POS and PPO copay plans, plus provide higher amounts than may be deposited into HSAs.

An HRA must be offered on a nondiscriminatory basis. Plan designs are generally limited to covering a portion of in-network services subject to deductible satisfaction. This is a significant difference versus funding HSAs, which do not include limitations, other than penalties and taxation, on how the individual may spend available funds. While HSA and FSA funds may be used to pay for out of network health care services, HRA funds are generally only available in network.

The option exists to allow unused HRA funds to rollover to the next year. While unusual, at times this makes sense, minimizing the need to increase the HRA amount if deductibles increase in future years.

As with FSAs, Sub Chapter S Corporation owners, directors and partners are not allowed to participate in a tax deductible HRA.

HRA plans are most appreciated when reimbursing the first half of an upfront deductible, maximizing positive plan perception as on average 75% of participants end up with $0 net out of pocket health care costs. Creative designs also reimburse a portion of the deductible up front, followed by a personal responsibility portion and then more in HRA reimbursements if claims costs are high enough.

At times the second half of a deductible is reimbursed along with out of pocket costs above the minimum legal qualified high deductible in a plan offering HSAs. HRAs in certain plans reimburse copays along with a portion of coinsurance responsibility.

Back filling "out of pocket" cost exposure maintains affordability and is efficiently achieved when HRAs are coupled with FSAs. One Debit card may be offered to access both HRA & FSA funds. When you know you will spend the entire deductible in health care expenses, having 100% of funds available on the Debit Card eliminates cash flow concerns and maximizes pre-tax payment efficiencies.

Health Reimbursement Account (HRA)

- **1st Dollar reimbursement of in-network deductible expenses**
- **Debit Card provided**
- **1st $1,250 individual**
- **1st $2,500 with dependents**
- **No Rollover of unused funds**
- **60% loss ratio**

HRA are offered at times instead of HSAs because:
- A. A projected 60% loss ratio allows employers to promise more money to offset deductible expenses than with HSAs.
- B. 100% of the promised HRA amount is available at time of need vs. HSAs where only on deposit amounts may be withdrawn.
- C. Expected "out of pocket" costs above the HRA may be deferred using a pre-tax FSA.

CY 2015	FSA	HRA	HSA
First available	1978	2002	2004
Funding	Flexible	Employer	Flexible
Plan Design	n/a	n/a	QHDHP
Max Deferral	$2,550	n/a	$3,350 S/ $6,650F
Catch up option	n/a	n/a	$1,000 ages 55+
Maximum Out-of-Pocket	n/a	n/a	$6,450 Single $12,900 Family
Rollover	2.5 months	Employer	Unlimited
Interest accrual	n/a	Employer	Yes
Portability	No	No	Yes
Taxation Section 213d	Pre-Tax Yes	Pre-Tax Yes	Pre-Tax Yes
Medicare & LTC	No	No	Yes except Medicare Supplement

V. Bargained Plans & Too Much Insurance

Unionized labor earns credit as a major force behind the founding of America's employer funded health insurance system. Wage controls to minimize inflation during World War II prompted bargaining for employer paid hospitalization. Winning this benefit for workers served America well then and confirmed the standard for employers investing in the health of its workers.

Now, only a few generations later, this laudable success is at the center of our ever increasing affordability problem. Little or no out-of-pocket cost insurance coverage to treat ailments is considered the Platinum standard. When available to patients an ever increasing volume of services and procedures are performed hyper inflating claims costs and leading to unsustainable premium increases.

Health care products and services relieve pain, neutralize symptoms and at times, especially in complex and sophisticated situations, are curative. The diagnosis of worrisome symptoms, especially for parents concerned for their children, is a priceless benefit. Health insurance is important so that if at some point in the future a loved one becomes ill, financial protection exists to cover the cost of health care treatment.

Evidence Based Medicine studies conclude that as much as half of health care services Americans receive may not be clinically necessary. People will use more health care if out of pocket costs are nominal. More services do not necessarily make us healthier. Health care providers act more defensively, motivated by malpractice concerns or profit if insurance pays the bills. If it doesn't personally cost us much, why not be certain and order all of the tests possible?

Well-intentioned union leaders bargain away wage increases to maintain rich health insurance benefits. Since decision makers are usually older than the average union member, the personal importance of generous coverage may be greatest to them and their spouses. Couple this with how our society focuses on short term desires and expectations. These end up being barriers versus embracing the advantage of longer term savings.

Younger members today will need more health care later, so fairness is not at issue. When bargaining includes funding Health Savings Accounts as a future standard, more members will be better served with costs not rising as quickly, with pre-tax efficiency in the purchase of health care services adding to take home pay.

The following charts show how pre-tax health care savings can grow even when funds are used every year for normal and, at times, high cost health care needs. No worker should be denied this opportunity as they are then shut out from winning the health care game.

HEALTH SAVINGS ACCOUNT GROWTH PROJECTION
INDIVIDUAL COVERAGE

AGE	DEPOSITS	USAGE	GROWTH @ 5%
45	$2,500	$1,500	$1,050
46	$2,500	$1,500	$2,153
47	$2,500	$1,500	$3,310
48	$2,500	$1,500	$4,526
49	$2,500	$1,500	$5,802
50	$3,000	**$3,000**	$6,092
51	$3,000	$1,750	$7,709
52	$3,000	$1,750	$9,407
53	$3,000	$1,750	$11,190
54	$3,000	$1,750	$13,062
55	$3,500	**$3,500**	$13,715
56	$3,500	$2,000	$15,976
57	$3,500	$2,000	$18,350
58	$3,500	$2,000	$20,842
59	$3,500	$2,000	$23,459
60	$4,000	**$4,000**	$24,632
61	$4,000	$2,500	$27,439
62	$4,000	$2,500	$30,386
63	$4,000	$2,500	$33,480
64	$4,000	$2,500	$36,729
65	$5,000	**$5,000**	$38,565
66	$5,000	$3,000	$42,594
67	$5,000	$3,000	$46,823
68	$5,000	$3,000	$51,264
69	$6,000	**$6,000**	**$53,828**

Assumes 5% compound interest earnings & maximum projected deferrals.

HEALTH SAVINGS ACCOUNT GROWTH PROJECTION
COVERAGE WITH DEPENDENTS

AGE	DEPOSITS	USAGE	GROWTH @ 5%
45	$5,000	$2,000	$3,150
46	$5,000	$2,000	$6,458
47	$5,000	$2,000	$9,930
48	$5,000	$2,000	$13,577
49	$5,000	$2,000	$17,406
50	$6,000	**$6,000**	$18,276
51	$6,000	$2,250	$23,127
52	$6,000	$2,250	$28,221
53	$6,000	$2,250	$33,570
54	$6,000	$2,250	$39,186
55	$7,000	**$7,000**	$41,145
56	$7,000	$2,500	$47,927
57	$7,000	$2,500	$55,049
58	$7,000	$2,500	$62,526
59	$7,000	$2,500	$70,377
60	$8,000	**$8,000**	$73,896
61	$8,000	$3,000	$82,841
62	$8,000	$3,000	$92,233
63	$8,000	$3,000	$102,095
64	$8,000	$3,000	$112,450
65	$9,000	**$9,000**	$118,072
66	$9,000	$4,000	$129,226
67	$9,000	$4,000	$140,937
68	$9,000	$4,000	$153,234
69	$10,000	**$10,000**	**$160,895**

Assumes 5% compound interest earnings & maximum projected deferrals.

VI. Medicare – When I'm 65 or maybe 70

American seniors are winners at the health care game having access to retiree health insurance coverage called Medicare that became law 50 years ago. It is also true that navigating health insurance options can be overwhelming when reaching the Medicare eligibility age.

The terminology is vexing. There are "Parts" in addition to "Plans." Some of the insurance is already paid for and some requires making payments until Social Security kicks in, then deducted from one's retirement check. It quickly comes to light that Medicare alone is not good enough on its own, resulting in the need to purchase supplemental, wrap around coverage, Prescription Rx insurance or enrollment in a Medicare Advantage plan.

Seniors purchasing a MediGap plan (wraparound - supplement), plus prescription Rx coverage, end up with four types of coverage. Three of the four require premium payments. The option of purchasing one Medicare Advantage plan results in one or two premium payments, and yet if you travel extensively or have a second home in a different state, you will be ill advised to enroll in Medicare Advantage due to the lack of network hospitals and doctors where you travel.

It may seem complicated, but like learning to press ten telephone numbers on the telephone versus seven, we all accept such changes over time.

Unknown by many younger workers is that Medicare Part B, which covers the cost of physician services, is a voluntary program. Monthly premiums for this coverage are typically deducted from Social Security benefit checks. There are five premium levels based upon income, ranging from just over $100 per month to more than $300 per person per month. Retiring couples must double these amounts to properly calculate their total monthly premium responsibility.

If one continues to work fulltime at age 65 for a business with fewer than 20 employees, Medicare Parts A & B act as primary insurance for hospitalization and physician services. If one works full-time for a larger employer, the employer's plan is primary, meaning it pays first. It may not be financially advantageous to sign up for Social Security and Medicare until retirement if employed at a larger employer and funding HSAs.

There is no penalty for delaying Medicare enrollment to a later time if working for a larger employer, as long as you maintain active worker coverage. COBRA health insurance continuation does not count and can result in future Medicare premium penalties.

Although dis-enrolling from an employer's plan is allowed, employers may not induce Medicare eligible workers to move to Medicare for their primary insurance. And it is almost never financially beneficial for a Medicare eligible worker to dis-enroll from their employer's plan and move to Medicare.

MEDICARE IS NOT RICH INSURANCE

Medicare Part A & B benefit levels are inferior to private health insurance. In 2008, the Medicare Part A deductible exceeded $1,000 for the first time, which equated to a 32% increase over the Calendar Year 2000 deductible of $776. The deductible rises almost every year climbing to $1,260 in 2015, 62% higher than in Calendar Year 2000.

Long term hospitalization under Part A is not covered at 100%, requiring significant payments per day. Costs after 60 days in hospital can exceed $8,000, and there is even greater exposure from 90 to 150 days, when out of pocket costs can exceed $35,000. This government coverage can even be exhausted.

The Affordable Care Act requires unlimited lifetime coverage for Americans under age 65 and limits out of pocket cost exposure to $6,600 single and $13,200 with dependents in 2015. Similar limits do not exist with Medicare.

Medicare Part B includes a nominal deductible around $150, but then requires 20% coinsurance forever; never transitioning to 100% coverage for physician services and diagnostic tests. A $10,000 physician expense results in $2,000+ in personal cost responsibility. These two realities are why most seniors purchase additional coverage.

Once retired, many seniors purchase a MediGap (wraparound / supplement) plan to pay some or all of what Medicare Part A & B does not pick up, such as deductibles and coinsurance. These "Plans" use a lettering system and are named Plans A though N. They are all offered by private insurers. Plans C & F are most popular because deductible and coinsurance costs are paid in full.

In 2006, prescription Rx plans under Medicare Part D became available for purchase. Part D Rx plans are sold by private insurers, who must offer government approved policies. Insurers generally offer two or three plan options.

The "Rx Hole in the Doughnut" concept, a brilliant solution to a challenging insurance coverage conundrum was included. It was too large though so the Affordable Care Act eliminates the doughnut hole by 2020, replacing it with 25% coinsurance.

Medicare Advantage plans are offered by private insurers as an alternative to Medicare A&B plus MediGap and are designed to include unlimited lifetime coverage protection. Most plans include copays for out of pocket costs. Some plans include dental, vision and hearing aid coverage or discounts at select providers.

MORE SAVINGS BY DELAYING MEDICARE
Once enrolled in Social Security, Medicare Part A coverage starts. The option to deposit pre-tax funds into a Health Savings Account then ceases. By delaying

enrollment in Social Security, benefit payments increase 8% annually and HSA contributions may continue. This will be a consideration as more and more Americans start winning the health care game.

With age 60 being the new age 40, it may be that the Medicare eligibility age will increase from 65 to 70 if born in 1960 or later. This change is likely to occur in concert with new private insurer plan designs with Medicare coverage that is more flexible and includes pre-tax health care savings opportunities.

MEDICARE FOR ALL
A "Medicare for All" system has been proposed by some as the answer to reigning in American health care spending. If such an approach takes hold, it will increase interest in supplemental health insurance.

Passing laws in our great country involves compromise. A "Medicare for All", or Single Payor System may lead to reduced access, rationing of care and a decrease in curative, technological investment and advancements. Hospitals and physicians end up entirely on the government's payroll, beholden to the bureaucratic expectations of standardized treatment protocols. Let's be realistic. This may be the future anyway with ACA.

Questions arise as to whether the greater good will be served in a "Medicare for All" system, as citizens in most other western countries already accept "one size fits all" government insurance. A little known fact is that private insurers act as government contractors processing all Medicare claims. The government takes the risk and insurance companies do the work.

Expect more changes when considering there are 80 million baby boomers transitioning towards retirement.

MEDICARE PART B, SUPPLEMENT & PART D Rx

AGE	PREMIUM +4% GROWTH	CUMULATIVE
65	$5,000	$5,000
66	$5,200	$10,200
67	$5,408	$15,608
68	$5,624	$21,232
69	$5,849	$27,082
70	$6,083	$33,165
71	$6,327	$39,491
72	$6,580	$46,071
73	$6,843	$52,914
74	$7,117	$60,031
75	$7,401	$67,432
76	$7,697	$75,129
77	$8,005	$83,134
78	$8,325	$91,460
79	$8,658	$100,118
80	$9,005	$109,123
81	$9,365	$118,488
82	$9,740	$128,227
83	$10,129	$138,356
84	$10,534	**$148,890**

49

People Stories for Winning the Health Care Game

Individuals, Couples and Family Decision - Making on Health Insurance Coverage

VII. *Single Ann's Wisdom Counselor*

For Ann, she felt like a winner and looked at it as her best investment of the year. Many of her co-workers made out just as well navigating through the company's new health insurance options.

Growing up, Ann's mother Helen worked two days a week in an insurance office. She was always in a great mood and made the tastiest meals after a day resolving claims issues for people. Ann did not know what it was about insurance that intrigued her, yet Mom always said, "You should pay for good insurance, because you never know when you will need it."

Ann, like most of us, had assumed the more expensive the health insurance plan the better. She then questioned this premise when her employer began promoting:

A. Plans with low payroll contributions and upfront deductibles
B. HRA & FSA pre-tax accounts to cover qualified health care expenses not paid by insurance
C. HSAs for long term savings
D. 100% catastrophic protection

When Ann went online to view the Open Enrollment information, she was intrigued by the upfront deductible plan being offered by her employer. Payroll deductions were much less than her current plan. This interested her because she and her fiancé were trying to save money for a down payment on a new home.

She then looked at the coverage details and was deflated. <u>Before the plan paid anything except wellness visits, she had to satisfy a $2,500 deductible!</u> The deductible applied to hospital stays, surgery, lab work, x-rays, office visits and even prescriptions.

Her perception improved as she read that her employer was offering to reimburse up to the FIRST HALF of the deductible in an HRA, or almost ONE THIRD in an HSA. It sounded interesting, but she was not certain the risk was worth it.

Ann brought up the new high deductible option during a visit with her mother at Helen's long term care facility. Ann's mother had retired a few years back after losing the use of her legs.

Helen's mind though was as sharp as ever. She read two newspapers a day, spent time online with her tablet computer, plus enjoyed a weekly business magazine. Helen was known to reference in conversation all kinds of articles about insurance, including Obamacare.

After Ann described the new plan option, Helen posed questions:

A. How much will you save next year in payroll deductions with the high deductible plan?

B. Can you estimate how much you will likely spend in copays?
C. Does your company offer a Flexible Spending Account?
E. Is the amount from your employer available through a Health Reimbursement Arrangement (HRA) or a Health Savings Account (HSA)?
F. Is the level of coverage 100% after the deductible has been satisfied, or are you responsible for 20% or more of ongoing bills?

Ann initially struggled to grasp the significance of these points as the concepts were new to her. She also knew her mother would be disappointed if she did not have the details by the time of her next visit.

First Ann compared her current plan's cost of $80 per pay to the upfront deductible plan at $30 per pay. Her pay would increase $1,300 per year if she chose the high deductible plan. Next she looked at copays this year for medical care, and figured out that four office visits cost $150 out of pocket, an x-ray of her wrist after slipping on the ice cost $150 out of pocket, and her prescriptions cost $300 per year. The total was $600.

Since her employer offered a voluntary Flexible Spending Account (FSA) program that allows pre-tax payment of out-of-pocket health expenses, she would have saved 30% in taxes equivalent to $160 if out of pocket copays had been funneled through an FSA. Ann also learned that the $1,250 from her employer was available through an HRA or she could have $800 deposited in an HSA that was not taxable.

During their next visit, Helen's first question kind of surprised her, and made her chuckle. Her Mom asked whether Ann had already decided on the new plan. "Why would I do that before seeking your advice, Mom?" she exclaimed. "Because you usually have your mind made up by the time you ask my opinion!"

"Well, I like the fact that I can reduce payroll deductions and increase my take home pay, and the maximum out of pocket cap of $5,000 is the same in both plans. I save on copays since the first half of the deductible is 100% reimbursed. It looks like I might save close to $2,000 if I change. But what am I missing? Isn't it too good to be true?"

"Do you understand that 20% coinsurance post deductible leaves you with another $2,500 in out of pocket risk? So worst case you could spend $3,750 if you have a major problem."

Ann responded, "The new plan has appeal the more that I study the details, especially since the odds are low that I will need high cost care. And the amount upfront will more than pay for the care I normally need.

"I'm actually surprised they call it a High Deductible Health Plan, since when you compound inflation, the purchasing power of $1,250 is equal to $125 about 30 years ago. And your decision?"

Qualified High Deductible Plan	In NETWORK	Out of NETWORK
	HRA: $1,250 SINGLE / $2,500 FAMILY or	
Benefits and Services	HSA: $800 SINGLE / $1,600 FAMILY	
Annual Deductible		
Individual	$2,500	$5,000
Family	$5,000	$10,000
After Deductible Plan Pays	80%	50%
Out of Pocket Limit		
Individual	$5,000	$10,000
Family	$10,000	$20,000
Lifetime Maximum	Unlimited	Unlimited
Preventive Care	100%, no Deductible	50%
Women's Health	100%, no Deductible	50%
Routine Physical	100%, no Deductible	50%
Routine GYN Exam	100%, no Deductible	50%
Well Child Care	100%, no Deductible	50%
Emergency Room	After Deductible, 80%	50%
Physician Office	After Deductible, 80%	50%
Specialist Office	After Deductible, 80%	50%
Chiropractic	After Deductible, 80%	50%
Inpatient Hospital	After Deductible, 80%	50%
Outpatient Hospital	After Deductible, 80%	50%
Maternity	After Deductible, 80%	50%
Surgery and Anesthesia	After Deductible, 80%	50%
Lab / X-Ray	After Deductible, 80%	50%
Physical Therapy	After Deductible, 80%	50%
Inpatient Psychiatric	After Deductible, 80%	50%
Outpatient Psychiatric	After Deductible, 80%	50%
Prescription Drugs	*After Deductible is Satisfied*	
Retail Rx	$10 Generic / $40 Preferred / $60 NP	
Mail Order Rx	$30 Generic / $80 Preferred / $120 NP	

"I have decided on the Upfront Deductible plan with the HRA. Worst case I am better off, and in a normal year way ahead. The entire $1,250 is available when needed using the HRA and the same is true for what I may deposit into the FSA.

I will save $500 in the FSA knowing if unspent it rolls over to the next year. Saving money to buy a house is more important now than for future health care costs. Someday I will want an HSA, but now protecting my cash flow is most important."

Helen felt a sense of thanks that her daughter made a winning decision. She scribbled down a comparison.

Current Plan:	$2,080 in payroll deductions
	$ 600 in expected copays
	$2,680 KNOWN COST
Additional risk:	$4,400 to out of pocket cap
Max Exposure	**$7,080**
New Plan:	$780 in payroll deductions
	$0 in deductible
	$780 KNOWN COST
Additional risk:	$3,750 to out of pocket cap
Total	**$4,530**
Expected Savings:	*$1,900*
Worst Case Savings:	*$2,550*

VIII. *Dave & Doris' Best Choice*

Ann's boss Dave was interested in the process she and Helen had gone through concluding that the Upfront Deductible plan as the better choice. His wife Doris and he had three teenage age children and recently celebrated 20 years of marriage.

Doris was in charge of the family's medical care needs. They rarely discussed health insurance at home, except for the hassles obtaining prescription approvals to treat the asthma of their youngest child. The copay for one medicine was $60 per month, which seemed like a lot until they found out its real cost was $180.

Their current plan for the family was increasing in cost to $200 per pay, or $5,200 per year. Deductions for the Upfront Deductible plan were $120 per pay, or $3,120 per year, a savings of $2,080. The deductible was $5,000 for the family, with the first $2,500 available from the company through an HRA or $1,600 deposited in a portable HSA.

Dave knew the asthma medicine alone cost $2,160 for the year, versus current copays of $720. Doris and he sat at the kitchen table after dinner one night and figured out their copay costs. The family used 6 maintenance medicines each month and averaged 12 office visit appointments. Since some of these were to treat sinus infections, antibiotics resulted in 3 additional prescriptions. They anticipated at least one emergency room visit and an x-ray, projecting $1,800 in copays.

Current Plan:	$5,200 in payroll deductions
	$1,800 in expected copays
	$7,000 KNOWN COST
Additional risk:	$8,200 to out of pocket cap
Max Exposure:	**$15,200**
New Plan:	$3,000 in payroll deductions
	$3,400 in deductible
	$6,400 KNOWN COST
Additional risk:	$5,000 to out of pocket cap
Max Exposure:	**$14,400**
Expected Savings:	*$600*
Worst Case Savings:	*$800*

The family knew they could easily spend the entire $5,000 deductible during a normal year, and have more out of pocket costs for prescription copays and coinsurance. But they still saved money with the Upfront Deductible plan by deferring an additional $3,400 in an HSA. Paying deductible and coinsurance costs with pre-tax dollars saved $1,000 in income taxes.

If they had a year that did not include any accidents or major illnesses, some HSA money would roll over to the next plan year. And fortunately they had an IRA they could tap into to transfer funds into the HSA if health care expenses were higher than expected. Changing offered the chance to win.

IX. *Invincible Charlie's Winning Choice*

Charlie believed Americans have the freedom to make choices, including whether or not to be insured for health care. He considered health insurance a luxury of our advanced society.

The routine is established with the birth of a child. Young parents visit the doctor to be certain their baby is healthy and comfortable. Pediatricians administer immunizations and measure reactions. Additional follow up care happens once teething infuriates the nasal passages. Nostril ooze may or may not mean there is a bacterial or viral condition. The pattern of "running" to the doctor has begun.

If we have limited or no consideration for the cost of a health care purchase because it is paid in full by insurance or society, our sensibilities about return on investment become skewed and lead to "use abuse." When knowledge about total cost is a factor, personal acceptance of the entire burden, both financial and physical is more likely to occur.

And then you have young guys like Charlie who believe they do not need health insurance. Why reduce their pay for protection when they rarely get sick? Clinics and hospitals can't turn anyone away is the thinking. At age 27 and accomplished in a variety of sports, Charlie especially loved skiing and club soccer.

Not being insured was risky, but so is life the way he looked at it. Charlie had historically declined health insurance coverage to have extra money for his sports adventures.

He was aware that with the new Obamacare law he could be fined or taxed for not being insured, but he had also heard that the penalty was less expensive than insurance he was not likely to use.

REALITY AS A WAKE UP CALL

It was the story about a buddy who wiped out on his bike and hit a tree that shocked him into thinking about signing up for health insurance. Charlie's friend got banged up so badly he ended up out of work for six months. His friend did not have health insurance and was now paying $250 per month for the next 10 years to pay off the cost of his care.

If people have to choose between spending money on food or medicine, the system is broken. This notion is often reviewed in news stories to reinforce that access to quality health care is a right. So then, what level of risk exposure is reasonable? The Affordable Care Act tells us just over $6,000 each year is about right.

Ultimately Charlie concluded that a plan that cost the fewest dollars had some appeal, should he ever crash after jumping off his favorite cliff at Snowbird® in Utah, even if it meant one less ski adventure. Here is his chart which Ann kindly prepared for him as he reminded her of her younger brother.

Current Plan:	$0 in payroll deductions
	<u>$0 in expected copays</u>
	$0 KNOWN COST
Plus	1% to 2.5% of income tax
Additional risk:	*EVERYTHING!*
New Plan:	$780 in payroll deductions
	<u>$0 in deductible</u>
	$780 KNOWN COST
Additional risk:	$3,750 to out of pocket cap
Total	**$5,050**
Expected Savings:	*ACA* Penalty Tax Savings & Peace of Mind
Worst Case Savings:	No Comparison

X. *Amy & Joe's Mature Analysis*

Dave told his co-worker Amy, executive assistant to the big boss that he was moving to the new plan. At first incredulous, she asked "You do well financially, why not buy the best?" He replied that saving for college tuition was a financial hurdle, so the family was always open to new ideas that could free up cash. "By the way, that Upfront Deductible option may be best for your husband and you!"

Amy had recovered from breast cancer three years prior and appreciated a lack of insurance hassles other than always paying copays. Now age 60, their macrobiotic cooking regimen had helped her husband Joe and her to lose weight, plus eliminated the need for cholesterol or blood pressure drugs. He was also 60 and loved the outdoors. Their children were grown and on their own.

Amy decided to heed Dave's advice and study the Upfront Deductible plan option. Her payroll deductions dropped from $180 per pay to $100 per pay, a savings of $2,080 per year.

The interesting part about the HSA idea included the ability to deposit $6,050 tax-free above the $1,600 provided by the employer into her own HSA bank account. They were old enough to qualify for the "catch-up" rule, allowing an additional $1,000 per year to be deferred from age 55 until enrolled in Medicare. Because unused HSA funds rollover, it offered them an opportunity to generate additional tax-free savings.

Assuming they remained healthy, by the time they retired, $50,000 in health care retirement savings could be available in addition to their 401k. A winner! Dave had given Amy the worksheet from Ann's mother.

Current Plan:	$4,680 in payroll deductions
	$ 320 in expected copays
	$5,000 KNOWN COST
Additional risk:	$9,680
Max Exposure:	**$14,680**
New Plan:	$2,600 in payroll deductions
	$0 in deductible
	$2,600 KNOWN COST
Additional risk:	$8,400 to out of pocket cap
Max Exposure:	**$11,000**
Expected Savings:	*$2,400*
Worst Case Savings:	*$3,680*

Joe liked that this new plan meant they no longer had to hassle with never ending copays. He understood the payment risk upfront the first year because the HSA money accumulated per pay. Fortunately they had a "rainy day" reserve in their savings account, so if a costly health care bill occurred prior to building the HSA, money was available to deposit into it. He also liked the concept of an emergency health care fund.

Amy and Joe respected that hospitalization is expensive. Chronic care needs can be very costly when you must return again and again for treatment, paying a copayment each visit, as she experienced after her breast cancer. They supported parts of the Affordable Care Act, since for the health care system to work efficiently patients should not have the risk of outrageous out of pocket costs for their care needs. At the same time people are becoming more aware of the true cost of quality health care.

Upfront Deductible plans offer premium savings versus copay plans for accepting reasonable risk, which can be neutralized. Simplicity in design enhances why this type of coverage is best over time for winning the health care game.

Take your own test on the following page by adding up what your family or just you will spend for health care needs next year. It may make sense to start saving for your future!

Sample Health Insurance Risk Analysis

Your Current Plan: $_____ in payroll deductions

$_____ in expected copays

$_____ KNOWN COST

Additional risk: $_____ to out of pocket cap

Max Exposure: $_____

New Plan: $_____ in payroll deductions

$_____ in deductible

$_____ KNOWN COST

Additional risk: $_____ to out of pocket cap

Max Exposure: $_____

Expected Savings: _____

Worst Case Savings: _____

Effectively Winning the Health Care Game

> "All truth goes through three stages.
> First it is ridiculed.
> Second it is strongly opposed.
> Third it becomes self-evident."
>
> ## 19th Century Philosopher Arthur Schopenhauer

XI. The New Way to Ask Your Doctor

Winners at the health care game think about how many doctor's office visits are diagnostic and curative, along with what percentage of the time a trip to the doctor is an "assurance" visit. Monitoring by physicians is important to a good cure and responding to your doctor questions critical to discovery and recovery. So it comes down being sensible to avoid redundancy.

Our physicians are licensed and trained to effectively "spend" health care dollars. They order tests, determine conditions and prescribe treatment solutions. Trusting them isolates medical problems, prompting correction and cure. Physicians are regarded as our brightest and most talented citizens. How fortunate we are for their dedication and trust.

Physician training is really expensive. Unlike most other Western nations where the government funds the cost of medical school, personal financing of tuition in America can lead to debt that is so high, repayment schedules last as long as a home mortgage.

Being a doctor is an intellectually challenging and often uncomfortable career, especially for care givers assisting patients at the end of their lives.

Doctors must be business people in order to thrive financially. They negotiate with families and hospital administrators, often working long hours in service for their patients. We expect these professionals to recommend solutions that maximize the quality of our health and we also expect them to be perfect.

Do doctors want 100% of the care they provide to be paid by insurance? Sit in a crowded primary care physician waiting room and consider how physicians transition from one patient to the next. They are not distracted by whether the patient or their health plan is paying the bill. Ultimately they know that most of the cost of running their practice will be paid by health insurance plans and so they delegate financial details to professional office administrators.

Self-pay is on the rise. It can be difficult to collect fees though from patients who pay for care themselves. As self-pay increases, the number of visits per patient declines. Logic follows that demand for services is a function of need and personal cost responsibility. Doctors understand that the demand for health care services increases as more people are insured.

The trend toward concierge medicine where patients pay fees upfront to their physician, who then reduces the number of people they serve, is a proven way to ensure prompt and immediate attention. It is also a luxury for those with the means to pay for it.

America needs our physicians to help control health care expenses. We unfortunately encumber them with significant malpractice concerns and cost, which promotes defensive medicine and excessive testing. There can be a fine line between malpractice and maloccurrence. Reasonable non-economic award caps should become a national standard to protect against mistreatment, paying for mistakes when care or the lack of it harms patients, with emotional reward caps.

We expect our doctors to treat us with great care and should be responsible partners in order to continue to receive the best and most efficient care.

> **Patient Awareness of the Actual Cost of Health Care Services Reduces Defensive Medicine Spending, Translating into Double Digit Premium Savings.**

XII. Charge Master Woes & Billing Reform

Billing reform has not been effectively addressed in the Affordable Care Act. Insurance companies negotiate discounts that can equal as much as much as 70% below the "charge" for a medical supply or service. Waiting weeks following a medical procedure to learn a charge and its discounted cost is common. Arguments offered by health care administrators justifying a confusing charge master system are bluntly bogus.

Real price transparency must expand to win the health care game, increasing awareness of the actual cost of health care services. This will allow patients to better consider the true value of services.

Insurance companies, doctors and hospitals have defended the importance of keeping private the details of secretive pricing agreements in the spirit of adhering to laws against price collusion and monopolization. While this risk exists with transparency, an opportunity for price competition is also engaged.

Maintaining a charge master (or charges roster) is a health care provider's obligation. Medicare originally paid providers a discounted amount determined from the charge master. The original Medicare payment approach was replaced in time by a flat fee system. And yet, maintaining an inflated charge master, or price list, has continued. Its sole function now is to overcharge the uninsured.

Inflated charges lead to outrageous discounts. Like a proverbial shell game, this pricing approach is similar to the Oriental rug store offering an 50% discount every day of the year, with no truth to their "full price" claim.

Retailers slash real prices 50%+ when going out of business. In health care, high discount levels are used by insurers to showcase their "negotiating efficiency" versus competitors. Winners see through this charade.

Think about a $160 charge for a $100 service equating to a 38% discount. Increase the charge to $175 while continuing to accept $100 and the discount jumps to 43%. No additional value is achieved except the perception of a higher discount percentage. The charge for a physician office visit may be $200 with the insurance company approving $120, or 60% of the charge. THIS IS CRAZY!

Patients have been known to conclude that their physicians are being "ripped off" by insurance companies when bills are heavily discounted. Such thinking is as corrupt as the charge master itself.

American health care's contorted payment approach benefits no one in the end, since services seem more expensive than they truly are. It also feeds a negative paradigm that prompts many patients to ignore bills from providers, adding to payment delinquency.

Although higher costs are often translated to mean greater value, the opposite can also be true. It should cost less to have an operation by a team of professionals who performs specific procedures repeatedly. Efficiencies in quality and cost will increasingly emerge with price transparency.

Consolidated, bundled billing for services and procedures may ultimately replace line by line "fee for service" billing standards due to ACA. There is ai new "Reference Pricing" approach that will hopefully continue to grow as a resolution to the current problem.

Comparison of cost may then become available based on quality, value and price, which is the standard in other businesses.

With the current charges master system and discount variability, true costs for care are often as clear as mud. Replacement with a reference pricing approach including mark ups versus what Medicare pays is just one idea to reform the system. Winning the health care game must include fundamental billing reform.

Actual 21st Century Charges & Discounts

Service	Charge	Approved	Discount
A. MRI	$ 1,803.00	$ 676.13	63%
B. Office	$ 313.00	$ 198.89	36%
C. Inpatient	$41,926.00	$15,722.25	62%
D. X-Ray	$ 398.00	$ 177.90	45%

XIII. The Economics of Health Care & Health Care Employment

In the United States, spending on health care is approaching $3 trillion annually representing almost 20% of the economy. Hospitals drive local economies as the largest single employer in many regions. And with 80 million baby boomers in or approaching retirement, opportunities abound for new investments.

This is big business! Normally price efficiency results as expenditures and demand grows, but this has yet to occur with health care. In fact the opposite is the norm with health care cost inflation as the front runner.

Our willingness to pay more and more for the latest health care innovation is supported by how insurance works. Shouldn't we assume that a $10,000 procedure for back pain is not good as the new $20,000 option?

Research and development is incentivized by the desire to make a profit along with increasing quality of life. Health care consumers are unable to react to true value. Costs spin out of control in the name of progress.

WHO MAKES THE DECISION
Our government collects so much in taxes earmarked for health care that it is the largest single payor to hospitals. But the government does not purchase actual health care services. It is physicians and each of us that purchase health care. The government and insurance companies are the third party payor.

Government mandates to insurance companies are designed to be in our collective best interest. We want the best health and immediate help when suffering. Affordability is the greatest challenge of our era.

ACCOUNTABLE CARE ORGANIZATIONS
Why is it that hospitals always seem to be building a new wing or parking garage? Economically, health care spending is important for job creation.

Universities benefit from training students to be future health care workers. Construction firms benefit from building new hospital buildings. Suppliers benefit from providing materials. And new hospitals move towards all private rooms to reduce infection rates.

The new term for networks of hospitals and doctor groups is ACO or Accountable care Organization. As demand for services grows until the aging baby boom generation passes on, these institutions will now deal with incentives and disincentives for desired efficiency.

By 2030 it is projected there will be 80 million Americans covered by Medicare, almost doubling its current size of 45 million in one half of a generation. Since baby boomers are living longer than their parents, a fall-off in demand may not occur until 2050. The good news that so many are living longer because of great health care, includes the tradeoff of an affordability tipping point.

How will we continue to invest greater resources in health care to promote job growth and overall quality of life? Let's get personal. What would you do if you knew a possible cure existed for your problem and it was only a matter of money to enhance your recovery chances?

This is a rhetorical question to reflect on why we will continue to see the business of health care grow. It is only a bad thing if our society declines in other ways because we devote excessive resources to health care.

THE ROLE OF GOVERNMENT
Legislators and policy makers affect health care in this country in many ways, including the formation of laws impacting taxation of health care and payments for health care services under Medicare and Medicaid.

Government initiatives also fund the advancement of our population's quality of health. It is a complex responsibility. The HMO Act of 1973 was approved at the end of the Nixon administration. It took ten years for the concept to become popular, but once accepted, health coverage changed for most Americans by reducing out of pocket risk along with provider selection freedom.

The Affordable Care Act includes goals for fixing our health care system by eliminating redundancies and making electronic medical records that track details increase the standard for efficiency. It also promotes health insurance plans with increasing out of pocket cost and premium responsibility to slow down usage.

XIV. Efficiently Winning the Health Care Game

The savvy will navigate here for reinforcement about winning the health care game. Minimizing premiums by accepting reasonable risk coupled with tax advantaged savings to pay for normal and future health care needs is the right, long term strategy.

We are evolving to a time when a saving will become a standard to afford retiree health care. Health Savings Accounts will increasingly be promoted alongside 401(k) / 403(b) plans and Individual Retirement Accounts (IRAs).

For Americans lacking the income or desire to save for retirement health care, drawing funds from an HRA and FSA offers efficient short term cash flow protection and a sense of consumerism, reducing unwarranted health care utilization.

In order to win the health care game, pre-tax "Account Based Plans" are necessary, married to health care plans with upfront deductibles. Deductibles give consumers pause to evaluate the merits of costly health care services. The logic of the investment becomes self-evident.

For almost all of us health care service needs are inconsistent over life's tenure. In good times, winners build savings as a bridge for times when there is a need for expensive care.

A qualified High Deductible Health Plan (HDHP) mandates that all services except preventive care are subject to an upfront deductible. Even low cost, high volume services like office visits and prescriptions are subject to deductible satisfaction. Copays and coinsurance may be part of these plans only after the deductible has been paid in full. These HDHPs allow for pre-tax deposits to HSAs. If offered with a deductible offsetting HRA, participants cannot also fund an HSA. This choice should be personal.

A popular hybrid design has upfront deductibles for expensive, less often utilized services. Copays are charged for high frequency physician office visits and prescriptions. These plans do not allow legal funding of HSAs, but may include an HRA and FSAs.

We appreciate having control over our finances and the freedom to make choices. Our savings potential with Upfront Deductible plans occurs after careful analysis of probable utilization of health care services. Utilization is defined as the quantity of health care products purchased and services performed. It all comes down to accepting <u>Reasonable Risk</u>.

An upfront deductible plan offers patients a credible reason to question not the doctor's diagnosis, but the testing or services that may be redundant, able to be procured later, or unnecessary. It also manages a leap of faith that catastrophic health care needs may occur in the future but are not tomorrow's reality.

The ability to save precious dollars for use on elderly health care costs promotes a lifetime savings desire versus a "use it up" spending mentality. Health care savings are like building equity versus renting. See the savings growth potential on pages 59 & 60.

Value standards for future health insurance purchases can be comparatively explained with an analogy about going out to dinner. The perceived value is different and better at a restaurant with fine service, linen table cloths and expensive entrées. Even though one can end up as full from food delivered through a window wrapped in paper, setting and cost connote value.

Nuances of value when dining can be compared with how many of us select a health insurance plan. But times have changed in that government approved coverage requires the same 100%, unlimited health care protection for high cost care regardless of plan choice. Less expensive premium plans are of the same quality except that normal care needs are shifted from an insurance expense to personal responsibility.

Let's review the accounts that offer pre-tax savings:

Health Savings Accounts (HSA) first became available in January 2004, and are now in use by more than 20 million Americans. HSAs require enrollment in a qualified High Deductible Health Plan (HDHP). HSA funds are the personal property of the account owner. Unused funds rollover. To encourage participation an employer may agree to fund a portion of HSAs and promote account owners to contribute their own pre-tax money through a Commitment Contract for building longer term savings. Because HSAs are portable, the funding expense to the employer is equal to 100% of the promised benefit.

Flexible Spending Accounts (FSAs) have been available since 1978. This voluntary benefit allows for the pre-tax payment of qualified health care products and services not paid by insurance, saving participants an average of $30 in taxes for every $100 deposited. Up to $500 in deferrals may be rolled to the next year. Awareness that 100% of the annual deferral is available in full at time of need adds to FSA popularity.

Health Reimbursement Arrangement (HRA)
Employers establish a self-insured plan that allows for the reimbursement of qualified medical expenses. HRA expenses must be entirely funded by the employer and are not portable. Depending upon the plan and employee turnover, the HRA loss ratio will be 30% to 80% of the promised benefit. The total annual benefit is available at time of need.

WHERE TO GO FROM HERE

To offset double digit premium cost increases, forward thinking employers have adopted "total replacement" Upfront Deductible Plans with the goal of economic beneficence for all participants, including lower income earners. Cost responsibility for one's health care needs must be properly balanced with life's other cost necessities. Upfront Deductible Plans are not meant to expose patients to expenses they cannot meet, but do require planning or acceptance of a relative "gusher" cost outlay versus copays that "drip" from our pockets.

Like a frog that slowly boils to its end as the water temperature rises, ever increasing premium costs for low out of pocket insurance erodes take home pay. With benefits being a form of compensation, including reasonable risk approaches is a winning, responsible course to balance cost and value.

We culturally accept allowing thousands of dollars in spending annually for lower income earners as long as the money "drips" out of out of individual pockets each day. It is the "gusher" expense of thousands of dollars that people with limited funds struggle to afford.

When it comes to health care, we often draw the line that risk exposure is wrong minded. This thinking is not logical based upon our inconsistent need for high cost health care services over time.

MOST EFFICIENT HEALTH PLAN OPTIONS
A proven and simple to understand strategy to meet the needs of participants at various income, cash flow and demographic levels includes:

1. A qualified HDHP with the option of HSAs and a <u>Commitment Contract</u> for funding amounts above employer deposits. Employer HSA deposits may be set equal to a projected HRA loss ratio, with half of the annual employer amount funded the first month,

and the balance deposited equally over the next 11 months. A limited FSA option is appropriately made available for dental, vision and post minimum medical deductible out of pockets expenses.
2. The same plan with the option of a first dollar HRA. Participants may also make voluntary deferrals to an FSA. This approach protects cash flow, since 100% of the promised HRA and FSA deferrals are available at time of need. HRA and FSA funds are conveniently loaded on one Debit Card.
3. A third option at increased payroll contributions is a hybrid Upfront Deductible plan with or without an HRA that includes office visit and prescription Rx copays. Copays are not subject to HRA reimbursement. A voluntary FSA is made available. This approach maintains consumerism for high dollar, lower volume health care services with desired copays for office visits and prescriptions.

Even though the initial analysis by many human resource and insurance professionals regarding this approach had been that it involves too much change and is not worth the "hassle", sensibilities are maturing.

A paradigm shift has taken hold as the approach is now respected for its long term economic efficiency. It is the way to win the health care game.

Upfront Deductible Plans are proven to reduce costs over time resulting in:
- Lower health care premiums
- Lower employee payroll deductions
- Pre-tax out of pocket costs
- Rollover of unused pre-tax funds
- Simplified plan designs
- Financial awareness of costs
- End to excessive utilization
- 100% upfront coverage then risk

The trajectory is building for these plans to become the new standard for comprehensive health insurance. Awareness of saving for future retiree health care needs is a welcome derivative of this trend, reducing worry about paying for future health care costs as we age.

Risk avoidance advocates who just don't care and want to keep it all simple, with health care needs mostly pre-paid, will hopefully remain able to purchase a new, expensive Cadillac each year. That will include a 40% surcharge on premiums above $10,200 single and $27,500 family coverage in 2018 due to the Obamacare "Cadillac Tax." The financial tide is rising against this traditional philosophy.

The right health insurance plan should balance payroll deductions with one's ability to afford medical services. Financial efficiency is about thresholds, including what we can and cannot afford to spend from take-home pay and savings.

Upfront Deductible Plans and health care consumerism prompts participants to make quality (not quantity) decisions about their medical care needs, increasing fiscal control over health care outlays. The cost curve is flattened and pre-tax savings are maximized. Results validate the effort as financial health improves without sacrificing personal health and winning the health care game.

"When considering health insurance options, a lower cost premium plan will be BEST when all factors and figures are analyzed & annualized, assuming it includes cash flow protection with pre-tax savings to pay current and future health care expenses."

BENEFITS GLOSSARY

ACCOUNT BASED PLANS – HSAs / FSAs / HRAs

ACCOUNTABLE CARE ORGANIZATION – Terminology describing hospital and physician conglomerates who accept risk in the care of patients, evolving away from fee for service revenue streams

ACQUISITION COST - The true wholesale cost for a health care product; what the provider or reseller pays to the manufacturer

BIO-METRICS – Wellness and prevention information obtained by testing blood, blood pressure, carbon monoxide, nicotine and body mass index

BROKER - Professional representing buyers of insurance rather than insurers

CAFETERIA PLAN – Benefit plan that offers the choice between cash or one or more tax favored options

CHARGE MASTER – A retail price list for all products, services and procedures provided by hospitals and physicians, also referred to as the "charges roster." These prices are dramatically higher than discounted amounts paid by the government and insurance companies

CHIP – Children health insurance plans available from a state

COBRA – Federal law allowing for the continuation of health benefits postemployment for 18 – 36 months, requiring beneficiaries to pay premiums

COMMITMENT CONTRACT – Voluntary agreement to achieve financial savings and rewards for funding HSAs, smoking cessation and improving Bio-Metrics

CONSUMER DRIVEN HEALTH PLAN – Insurance coverage that includes upfront deductibles and other incentives to engage participants to consider the cost of healthcare services, resulting in the elimination of excessive utilization

COINSURANCE – Plan provision where the insured and the plan share a percentage of the cost of services (80% paid by the plan & 20% by the patient)

COORDINATION OF BENEFITS (COB) – Plan provision designed to eliminate duplicate payments for the same service when an insured is covered under two plans

COPAY – Flat dollar payments that are the responsibility of employees to pay a portion of the cost of a service ($20 / $40 / $60)

DEDUCTIBLE – Upfront out-of-pocket expenses that are the patient's responsibility before the insurance plan pays for services ($500 / $1,000 / $2,000 / $3,000)

ELIGIBLITY PERIOD – The number of days post-employment an individual must wait in order to obtain benefits coverage (90 days for example)

EVIDENCE BASED MEDICINE – A scientific method for assessing the risk and merits of health care treatments, based upon historical data

FIDUCIARY – Individual(s) who act in a capacity of trust and exercise discretionary authority over the management of an employee benefit plan

FLEXIBLE SPENDING ACCOUNT (FSA) – Employee per pay deferrals that allow the purchase of qualified health and dependent care services pre-tax up to a $500 annual rollover

HEALTH CARE EXCHANGE – Government managed online system for purchasing health insurance that may include subsidies to establish net premium cost based upon income. Plans are offered by private insurers and labeled Platinum, Gold, Silver, Bronze & High Deductible

HEALTH MAINTENANCE ORGANIZATION (HMO) – A pre-paid medical plan designed to limit access to specific providers for good health while minimizing costs

HEALTH REIMBURSEMENT ARRANGEMENT (HRA) – An employer provided benefit designed to offset a portion of deductibles, allowing a rollover of unused funds option

HEALTH RISK ASSESSMENT – A wellness program questionnaire designed to promote awareness of health risk factors, sometimes referred to as a Health Risk Assessment

HEALTH SAVINGS ACCOUNT (HSA) – Employee owned bank account allowing pre tax deposits to pay qualified health care expenses. Ability to make deposits requires enrollment in a qualified High Deductible Health Plan

HIPAA – Federal law passed in 1996 establishing privacy and non-discrimination standards

MANAGED CARE – An approach to health care cost containment popular in the late 20th and early 21st centuries

OUT-OF-POCKET MAXIMUM – Patient personal cost responsibility for covered health expenses

OPEN ENROLLMENT – The time period usually up to 60 days prior to a new plan year to make coverage choices

PATIENT PROTECTION & AFFORDABLE CARE ACT (PPACA) – Healthcare reform law that became March 23, 2010. Also referred to as the "Affordable Care Act" & "Obamacare."

PAY OR PLAY – Describing an employer's decision to offer health insurance to employees, or pay government penalties

PLAN DOCUMENT – ERISA qualified written description of plan coverage including employee rights

PLAN SPONSOR – The employer that establishes and maintains employee benefit plans

POINT OF SERVICE PLAN (POS) - A pre-paid medical plan like an HMO that includes out of network coverage

PREFERRED PROVIDER ORGANIZATION (PPO) – A network of providers offering discounts on a fee for service basis, allowing freedom of choice & out of network coverage

SELF INSURED – Benefit plans provided by employers who cover enough employees to pay for services as rendered, plus maintain their own reserves

STOP LOSS INSURANCE – Employer purchased coverage to limit catastrophic claim exposure for a self-insured medical plan

SSNRA – Social Security Normal Retirement Age access to government benefits at age 67 for persons born in 1960 and later

SUMMARY OF BENEFITS COVERAGE (SBC) – Eight page breakdown of health coverage features per government standards

SUMMARY PLAN DESCRIPTION (SPD) – Benefits booklet providing plan details

THIRD PARTY ADMINISTRATOR (TPA) – Specialized claims processor for self-insured plans

UPFRONT DEDUCTIBLE PLAN – Health insurance coverage with low premiums and a high deductible to be satisfied prior to payments by an insurance company

USUAL, REASONABLE & CUSTOMARY – Prevailing charges from similar providers for health care services

Online Resources

Jon's BLOG thehealthcaremind.com

1. IRS on FSA HRA & HSAs www.irs.gov/pub/irs-pdf/p969.pdf

2. US Center for Medicare & Medicaid Services www.cms.hhs.gov/

3. Patient Protection and Affordable Care Act www.dol.gov/ebsa/healthreform

4. International Foundation of Employee Benefit Plans www.ifebp.org/

5. Kaiser Family Foundation   www.kff.org

6. Cardio Kinetics   www.cardiokinetics.com

7. Well Score www.continuancehealthsolutions.com

8. Health Affairs   www.healthaffairs.org

8. DataPath   www.dpath.com

9. JP Warner Associates, Inc. www.warnerbenefits.com

10. Warner Benefits, Inc. www.warnerbenefits.net

11. Human Resource Administrators, Inc. www.hradministrators.com

Jonathan Pierpont Warner, CEBS

Combining a strong analytical focus and technical prowess, Jon Warner shines as a detail oriented, calmly confident and spirited communicator. These style characteristics differentiate him in his field.

In the maze of rising health care costs and legislative uncertainty, Jon illustrates strategic solutions that stand out as logical, caring and practical. Jon consults for large, complex, multi-site self-insured employers across a breadth of businesses. His approach is also adaptable for mid-size and smaller groups. Recommendations are delivered with creativity that is respectful of the unique culture characteristics of organizations.

His powerful leadership experience, engaging speaking style and calm confidence make him sought after for contract negotiations, consulting projects and public speaking events for prestigious organizations and non-profit groups.

Jon looks at health insurance in a contemporary light both philosophically and financially as the author of _How to Win the Health Care Game_ and the condensed _Winning the Health Care Game_. His 2009 book title is _Making Sense of 21st Century Health Insurance Plans_.

Owner of JP Warner Associates and co-owner of Warner Benefits with his brother Andrew, Jon also owns Human Resource Administrators, a Third Party Administrator (TPA) delivering administration processing solutions including HRA, HSA, FSA, Plan Document and COBRA services. His corporate awareness of how each of these tools integrates with wellness focused employee benefits strategies inures favorable benefits plan perception while controlling costs.

A Certified Employee Benefit Specialist (CEBS), Jon is a graduate of an intensive educational program developed by The International Foundation of Employee Benefit Plans and the Wharton School of the University of Pennsylvania. He has maintained his "Fellowship" status with this organization since 2002. Prior schooling included Moravian Academy and Liberty High School in Bethlehem, PA before graduating from Phillips Academy in Andover, Massachusetts. Jon holds a BA in Political Science from Middlebury College in Middlebury, Vermont.

Married for almost three decades, Jon and his wife Vicki have enjoyed raising three wonderful children while living in the western suburbs of Philadelphia, PA. Jon enjoys golf, skiing and singing as favorite activities. His devotion to education includes serving as Chairman of the J. Wood Platt Caddie Scholarship Trust offering college tuition assistance to golf caddies, as a Trustee for the Country Day School of the Sacred Heart in Bryn Mawr, PA, and as an alumni interviewer for prospective Middlebury College students.

Jon is also a certified alpine ski instructor (retired) and has been a member and Trustee for the Philadelphia Boys Choir & Chorale. Along with his son he has appeared live on ABC's Good Morning America, in addition to singing and touring on four continents. He is a member of the C12 Group of Christian business owners and CEOs, which inspired him to complete his goal to author books explaining American health insurance history and legislative trends allowing financially efficient insurance protection and savings.

www.ingramcontent.com/pod-product-compliance
Lightning Source LLC
Chambersburg PA
CBHW051549170526
45165CB00002B/938